G000296098

*Especially for*

.......................................................................

*From*

.......................................................................

*Date*

.......................................................................

ISBN 978-1-63058-736-9

Published by Barbour Books, an imprint of Barbour Publishing, Inc., P.O. Box 719, Uhrichsville, Ohio 44683, www.barbourbooks.com

*Our mission is to publish and distribute inspirational products offering exceptional value and biblical encouragement to the masses.*

 Member of the
Evangelical Christian
Publishers Association

Printed in China.

A Devotional Journal

# When *Jesus* Speaks
## to a
## Mother's Heart

### Shelley R. Lee

## BARBOUR BOOKS
An Imprint of Barbour Publishing, Inc.

# I AM

*Jesus said to them, "Truly, truly, I say to you,*
*before Abraham was born, I am."*
JOHN 8:58 NASB

Yes, I said these words when I walked the earth, and it really stirred things up! People weren't expecting a common man like Me; they were looking for a kingly type. And, well, you likely know that I am the King, but this seemed blasphemous to many of them at the time.

My Father, the Holy Spirit, and I make up the triune God. We are One. I was there at creation and all along with My Father. I know it can be hard for the human mind to grasp, but the Holy Spirit will help you begin to wrap your mind around this and many other things.

As a mother you are especially in need of His guidance. You know that so much is riding on how you parent your precious children. I don't need to tell you that. You love them inexplicably! I want you to know that I love them and you even more!

It's pretty impossible to comprehend the depth of My love, but parenting comes close. It's the closest look you'll get this side of heaven, and I want to help you do your very best—beyond your best, actually. Because I am the One who can fill any gaps you may have in parenting.

*God, how I need You in my giant job as a mother.*
*Help me to listen to Your Word and Your guidance. Amen.*

# THE REAL ENEMY

*For we do not wrestle against flesh and blood, but against the rulers, against the authorities, against the cosmic powers over this present darkness, against the spiritual forces of evil in the heavenly places.*
EPHESIANS 6:12 ESV

There are many dark things woven into your life on different levels, many that you don't even recognize yet. Let Me encourage you with important truth right where you are.

Remember that the battle is spiritual. No matter how much it may seem at times that people are against you, the root of all trouble and opposition to what is good and true is always the Enemy of your soul. He seeks to destroy you and your children in any way he can.

Be super alert, like a neighborhood watch over your heart and over everything that regards your children. Never forget, I am the all-powerful Victor! No matter how overwhelmed you may feel, keep in mind that I am far bigger.

Pray. Talk to My Father and Me frequently (Ephesians 6:18 MSG) about whatever you are facing or fearing. There is tremendous power in prayer. You are so dear to Me, My Father, and the Holy Spirit. We've got your back!

*Father God, my family and I are depending on You today. Thank You for being my Protector, Defender, and Warrior in the raging spiritual battles that I am oft unaware of. You are so good to me! Amen.*

# HOPE FOR TODAY

*I would have despaired unless I had believed that I would see
the goodness of the LORD in the land of the living. Wait for the LORD;
be strong and let your heart take courage; yes, wait for the LORD.*
PSALM 27:13–14 NASB

My dear child, I know the things that cause you to despair in this earthly life—deeply, at times.

You know you have the promise of eternal life without decay or death of any kind, but I want to give you hope for right now, too. I will show My goodness to you and your children in this life, today. I will not wait for eternity to bless you—of that you can be sure! Be patient.

This day, be strong in what you know. Be brave and do the right things. Remember, these are much simpler than many people think, like responding lovingly to your child when he makes a mistake or comforting him when he's afraid. Care for your child physically and spiritually in every small way you can think of today.

My goodness is going to come to you.

*Lord God, thank You for the hope You give me for this
day and each day into eternity. Strengthen me to be all
I can for You and for my children today. Amen.*

# HEAVY LIFTING

*"Come to me, all who labor and are heavy laden, and I will give you rest. Take my yoke upon you, and learn from me, for I am gentle and lowly in heart, and you will find rest for your souls. For my yoke is easy, and my burden is light."*
MATTHEW 11:28–30 ESV

Your burdens for your children are tremendous at times, and rightly so. Their lives are precious, and you have a weighty job being their mother!

It may sound cliché, but I really do want to take your burdens.

You have so much to juggle; I watch you. You care for your little ones and do so many things at the same time. You'll have laundry going while dinner is cooking. Meanwhile, you'll get a Band-Aid for one and water for another, pick up toys, settle an argument, set the table, and update the family calendar. All the while, there are bigger burdens than daily, routine things—the ones that feel like a lead vest. The good news is that I want to lighten all of this for you. Hand over all of it; let Me do all I know you need help with. I'll give you a light load that you can walk with through the day and feel good about.

*Lord, help me to give over my burdens to You. Provide the relief and rest I need to be the best I can be for the children You've entrusted to me. Amen.*

# LIMITLESS LOVE

*For I am convinced that neither death, nor life, nor angels, nor principalities, nor things present, nor things to come, nor powers, nor height, nor depth, nor any other created thing, will be able to separate us from the love of God, which is in Christ Jesus our Lord.*
ROMANS 8:38–39 NASB

I f I could articulate this in person to you right now, I would shout from the top of the nearest hilltop where you and a lot of other people could hear Me loud and clear, "I *love* this woman! I *love* her!" And of course I would be pointing at you the whole time.

I am not sure you realize that there isn't a single thing you can do that could keep Me from loving you like this. No behavior, no attitude, no bad decision. No evil act by another, no loss, no hidden past. Nothing.

No poor judgment as a mother. No yelling rant. No abandonment. There is literally nothing you have done, do, or will do that will keep Me from loving you.

I love you, and I always will. My love changes your life. It makes you the mother you want to be, the person you want to be.

I love you!

*Lord, help me remember Your eternal, undying love for me, that I may grow in it and shine Your love on my children. Amen.*

# GROW YOUR PASSION

*For where jealousy and selfish ambition exist, there is disorder and every evil thing. But the wisdom from above is first pure, then peaceable, gentle, reasonable, full of mercy and good fruits, unwavering, without hypocrisy.*
JAMES 3:16–17 NASB

When you are tempted to be jealous of someone else's abilities and circumstances, I want you to remember something. You have been made with a special set of abilities and attributes that are fitted for a wonderful purpose in the life where you are, as well as where you are going!

You may think this is just something Christians say to feel better about their place in life, but I'm very serious about this. Looking at other mothers who you perceive have a better life or skill set than yours will lead to many false thoughts and ideas. It will hinder your relationships and your self-image.

You know what you love, where your passion is. I will give you the wisdom to grow in your strengths. So keep asking Me, and keep growing. You are a beautiful mother, and you're growing more beautiful all the time.

*Dear Lord, thank You for the strengths You have given me. Show me how to grow in them, that I may serve You exceedingly well. Amen.*

# KEEP LOOKING UP

*A cheerful disposition is good for your health;*
*gloom and doom leave you bone-tired.*
PROVERBS 17:22 MSG

Life is full of challenges as a mother, and you can be sure that I see them all. Thankfully there are many wonderful things, too, and even when it doesn't feel like it, they outweigh the tough ones. Your children are gifts as well as all that is provided for you to care for them. On top of that, there is the beauty of creation that is everywhere. Check it out!

If you keep looking at the positive things and keep your focus there, you will have a better outlook on life. As a side effect, the toxic energy produced by negativity will be absent from your body and will you have better health.

I'm not saying you shouldn't acknowledge the hard things in life; of course not! You must face difficulties to move through them. You will definitely walk through very low spots on your way to better places; the key is to not hang out there. No camping in the valley, that's the idea.

Keep looking up, and concentrate on what is good. I'm leading you to great places!

*Lord, thank You for all that is good in this day and in my life.*
*You have blessed me. Help me to count the many ways! Amen.*

# THE GREATEST WORK OF ALL

*But my life is worth nothing to me unless I use it for finishing*
*the work assigned me by the Lord Jesus—the work of telling*
*others the Good News about the wonderful grace of God.*
ACTS 20:24 NLT

The work you have as a mother sharing the Gospel of grace with your children is powerfully and eternally significant. You have the opportunity to change their lives here on earth and forever!

Remember this—your work is vital. Don't underestimate or short-sell the potential impact of simply sharing and shining My love every day.

Each opportunity you have to show grace and teach mercy, do it. Tell them all about Me. How I died that they might have life. How I am with them always. How they can know Me personally, just like you. You will be surprised how much their young hearts understand.

Keep growing and glowing in My love. The effect your family can have on those around you will be amazing. It is something I love to see!

*Dear God, give me the grace and strength I need to extend the same*
*grace You offer me to my children, that they may know You. Amen.*

# HINDRANCES

*Therefore, since we are surrounded by such a huge crowd of witnesses to the life of faith, let us strip off every weight that slows us down, especially the sin that so easily trips us up. And let us run with endurance the race God has set before us.*

HEBREWS 12:1 NLT

What is it that weighs you down in your faith walk? What keeps you from being the best mother you can be?

I can see what it is, but you have to see it for yourself for it to make a difference for you.

Look to Me; I can help you see clearly, and I can help you clear away the roadblocks in your path.

So tell Me what you see that is hindering you. Is there unforgiveness? Unrealistic expectations? Are there lies you need truth to dispel? Is there a sin habit that is entangling you? Whatever it is, remember that I want to help you with this.

There's a great run ahead for you!

*Lord God, give me eyes to see the hindrances in my way, and then help me to lay them aside. These things are way too big for me. I need Your help. Amen.*

# SWIFT GRACE

*Be angry, and yet do not sin; do not let the sun go down on*
*your anger, and do not give the devil an opportunity.*
EPHESIANS 4:26–27 NASB

There are things in the day to day as a mother that can get you very upset. Sometimes it's your children who have done things; other times it's other children, or worse—their parents (they are human, just like you!). Try to remember that handling anger is nothing new, and you can get through it without losing control. I promise.

Though you may tremble with emotion at times, don't let it get ahold of you. Forgive swiftly rather than holding a grudge. If it's your children, discipline fairly and help them see you still love them no matter what. Learning and practicing to forgive others quickly, the way I forgive you, is a wonderful exercise that will make you stronger.

Before you go to sleep each night, talk to Me. I can help you see who you need to forgive so your heart isn't darkened in any way.

*Lord, bring to mind for me those I've held things*
*against, and help me to forgive them. You are the*
*Master of forgiveness. Show me the way. Amen.*

# THE PEACE RULE

*And let the peace of Christ rule in your hearts, to which
indeed you were called in one body. And be thankful.*
COLOSSIANS 3:15 ESV

S o much that is unsettling can settle in around you. In the midst of it all, I want you to know that the peace I give to you can empower you entirely. My peace can reign beautifully over your heart.

You can face everything that weaves its way into your world today, not only as a mother but in every role in the unique life that is yours.

When just a hint of unrest threatens to disrupt you, remember to lean into Me. Trust Me. This peace that I'll give you is an indescribable steadiness that you can get nowhere else. Not anywhere!

I made this world, and I know how to help you through it, even now in its fallen state.

I've watched you try to find peace by worldly means, but you know now how it just doesn't work. I long to bless you in many ways, and I will, but real peace can only be found in Me. I offer it to you now and always.

◇◇◇◇◇◇◇◇◇◇◇◇◇◇◇◇◇◇◇◇◇◇◇◇◇◇◇◇◇◇◇◇◇◇◇

*Lord God, let Your sovereign peace fill my heart and
my entire presence today. I need You every minute
in this complex life, Lord. I need You! Amen.*

# TRUTH STOREHOUSE

*Let the word of Christ dwell in you richly, teaching and admonishing one another in all wisdom, singing psalms and hymns and spiritual songs, with thankfulness in your hearts to God.*

COLOSSIANS 3:16 ESV

There will be times when you are incapacitated. You've already experienced some of them, like when you gave birth to your child or when you have been ill. During these stretches of time, you may not be able to be in My Word like you want to or should.

I want you to keep storing up My Word in your heart and mind. Let it fill every empty space you can manage. Not only will this help you when you are at full-functioning capacity as a mother and in every other role, but when you enter these times of incapacity, you will also have a reserve of truth and spiritual food to keep going. I will always provide for you and strengthen you when you need it, but if you do this, you are more likely to be able to minister to your children and others around you in a time of weakness for yourself.

So do it! Store up My Word; it's a treasure. Then just wait and see what I will do!

*Lord, bless this day with Your truth that will remain in my heart. Help me to remember it when it is needed to help me or someone else You put in my path. Amen.*

# FINISHING WHAT WE STARTED

*And I am sure of this, that he who began a good work*
*in you will bring it to completion at the day of Jesus Christ.*
PHILIPPIANS 1:6 ESV

We started something with you, My Father, the Holy Spirit, and I. You didn't see the beginning of it, but I did, and the whole thing is so beautiful! First, let Me go back a ways. We created you, and wow, We were so excited about the gifts We gave you and how wonderfully you were made! Then the Holy Spirit started to move in your midst and in your heart. I loved watching the whole process.

The great thing is that the work in you just keeps going.

So when you are discouraged about how things are going with your big assignment as a mother, remember this: I am committed to completing the work I started in you. You can count on it!

What's more, I am doing the same thing for your children. The work just keeps on going. So be encouraged; I am not done yet!

*God, thank You for the work You continue to do in me*
*and in my children. I am grateful for Your faithfulness to me.*
*Help me to be faithful in return to serve You well. Amen.*

# GUARD THE DOOR

*For though we walk in the flesh, we are not waging war*
*according to the flesh. For the weapons of our warfare are not*
*of the flesh but have divine power to destroy strongholds. We destroy*
*arguments and every lofty opinion raised against the knowledge*
*of God, and take every thought captive to obey Christ.*

2 CORINTHIANS 10:3–5 ESV

You feel the things that come against you and your children. You know they are there, but things can get dark and confusing very quickly, and you may at times feel powerless against the Enemy of your soul.

I want you to know that you have divine power through Me. With spiritual alertness and prayer, so much can be defended and conquered. Start at the door of your mind. Whenever an untrue or doubtful thought tries to get in, bring it to Me. I will help you sort it out, and this way you can get rid of lies and deceit before they grow in your mind with other thoughts.

The Enemy works in subtle ways, so be watchful and prayerful. Remember where your power comes from and that I am with you always!

*Lord God, give me discernment today over my thought*
*life. Bring truth to the forefront, that my children*
*and I will not be deceived by the Enemy. Amen.*

# REMEMBER

*The lines have fallen to me in pleasant places; indeed,
my heritage is beautiful to me. I will bless the LORD who has
counseled me; indeed, my mind instructs me in the night.
I have set the LORD continually before me; because
He is at my right hand, I will not be shaken.*

PSALM 16:6–8 NASB

Where I have placed you is no accident! Many have come before you in both your natural and your faith families, and you are right where you should be in all of it. I get very excited thinking about the impact you can have as a mother and in all the circles you are a part of!

I want you to celebrate the good moments and live with thanksgiving in those days. I love to bless you.

There are times when I know things can get really complicated, when it all feels like a big wreck. Try to remember it's a beautiful collision that I am going to do something spectacular with. I promise.

In all that happens with you and your children, the goodness that came before you and that is coming abounds with magnificence. I wish I could give you a mental download of it all, but little by little is best. Just remember.

*Dear God, thank You for the beauty of Your master plan and
that You have a special place for me in it all. Strengthen
me for the piece of it that will unfold today. Amen.*

# DEPENDABLE HELPER

*No test or temptation that comes your way is beyond the
course of what others have had to face. All you need to remember
is that God will never let you down; he'll never let you be pushed past
your limit; he'll always be there to help you come through it.*

1 Corinthians 10:13 msg

When your children push all your buttons and the people you care about the most let you down—these are just two instances when you are tempted to turn the wrong way. But I will help you through every tempting, testy time you experience.

You may feel like you will break under the pressure, for it can be great, but it will never be greater than your limit—because I am with you!

The Enemy will want you to feel guilty for just being tempted, but I want you to know if you keep seeking My help in these times, you have no guilt. You have victory! Stay with Me; I'll see you through.

---

*Lord, give me a knee-jerk reaction, whenever I am tempted,
to turn immediately to You for help. I need You, Lord, so I don't
fall into the many temptations that come my way. Amen.*

# KEEP ON PRAYING

*This is the confidence which we have before Him, that,
if we ask anything according to His will, He hears us. And if we
know that He hears us in whatever we ask, we know that
we have the requests which we have asked from Him.*
1 JOHN 5:14–15 NASB

I know there are things you have asked for and have received a big fat "no" or "not now" as an answer. That's hard. I know.

I want to encourage you! My Father knows exactly what you need and what is the very best for you. He will not do anything that is not going to be in your best interest, and not just for right now either. He has all of eternity in mind for you, and your children, too.

Don't let this stop you from going to Him with your requests—not one bit! Keep up the prayers! He hears every single one—you can be sure of that. Each utterance on behalf of your children, whether spoken or thought, yelled or whispered. Every request cried out in tears, and in joy, too.

Just trust that He will give you and your kids the absolute best. He will.

*Dear God, even when I don't understand the whys of
unanswered prayers, help me to trust You entirely. Amen.*

# KEEP ON KEEPIN' ON

*Let us not become weary in doing good, for at the proper
time we will reap a harvest if we do not give up.*
GALATIANS 6:9 NIV

Tired? I see how worn out you can become, and I want to cheer you on!
You can do this.

You get dog tired sometimes, doing all the right things in hundreds of
ways every day for your children and those you love. I see that. There is joy
in it for you, but it can all get absolutely exhausting. I see that, too!

I will strengthen you; just ask Me. But I want you to take the rest you
need, care for yourself well, and keep on going in your good fight. It may
be hard to believe, but amazing, miraculous things are going to come of
your efforts, just you wait and see! The blessings of your tenacious labor
on behalf of your children, especially, will be beyond what you can possibly
imagine right now. Trust in Me. It is going to be spectacular!

*Lord God, I need You to give me the strength to keep going in what is
good and true. I have so much to do and so many demands.
Thank You that You know them all. Give me all
that I need today. Amen.*

# A MILLION CHANCES TO SHOW GRACE

*Use your heads as you live and work among outsiders.*
*Don't miss a trick. Make the most of every opportunity. Be gracious*
*in your speech. The goal is to bring out the best in others*
*in a conversation, not put them down, not cut them out.*
COLOSSIANS 4:5–6 MSG

When you interact with those who don't know Me, I want you to be wise, gracious, and loving. Remember that I love every single person you bump into, whether it's your neighbor or your child's friend, that friend's family member, or maybe your child himself who needs Me. Reflect My love for them.

I will give you many opportunities to do this. Affirm the good in each person whenever you have the chance. Don't make them feel like your project; just enjoy them like you do your good friends. Include them in your life so that they can see the blessings of living a life of faith. But remember, just be gracious and kind. You'll notice that I repeated Myself. I'm glad you noticed! Be gracious.

*Lord, fill me with Your grace today, that I may be a mirror of it*
*for others I encounter. I want to shine for You, God! Amen.*

# MAKING IT MATTER

*Yet you do not know what your life will be like tomorrow.*
*You are just a vapor that appears for a little while and then*
*vanishes away. Instead, you ought to say, "If the Lord*
*wills, we will live and also do this or that."*
JAMES 4:14–15 NASB

Y ou know that eternity with Me is a sealed deal if you indeed know Me as your Savior. But there are no guarantees from one day to the next in this earthly life for you or your children. It's all very fragile, and that's easy to forget in the busyness of it all, isn't it?

With that in mind, make this day count for all you can. Do what you can with all that you have been given, and know that whatever happens, I am with you in it. Nothing surprises Me either, by the way! Keep looking up. Between My Father, the Holy Spirit, and Me, you know the triune God has you covered.

No matter how long the lives of you and your children are, they are short in the scope of eternity—and at the same time, eternally significant and precious.

*Lord God, give me eternal perspective in this day that is*
*but a breath. I need You to make it matter. Amen.*

# MIRACULOUS MYSTERIES

*But as for me, I will hope continually, and will praise You yet more and more. My mouth shall tell of Your righteousness and of Your salvation all day long; for I do not know the sum of them.*
PSALM 71:14–15 NASB

Since I have been fully man, I know the limitations of understanding God from your perspective. It's. . .well, impossible really! It can be relatively easy to thank and praise God and Me for My sacrifice that brought salvation, but the mysteries of it are immense.

On the subject of Our righteousness, you can get the concept that God is perfect and fallen man needed My sacrifice to make friendship with God possible. But I'm telling you, My Father is so magnificently righteous it would blow you away!

And while you can see many of the things We are doing on behalf of you and your children, there is so much that is being done that you cannot see. It's beyond comprehension in the earthly state you are in. All you need to know is that amazing things are being accomplished in My Father's master plan, and you are a benefactor of all of it!

*Lord, thank You for all You have done and are doing for me and my children. I can only begin to count it all. I rest in the mystery of Your miraculous work in the life of my family today. Amen.*

# SO MUCH GOOD TO THINK ON

*Finally, brethren, whatever is true, whatever is honorable, whatever is right, whatever is pure, whatever is lovely, whatever is of good repute, if there is any excellence and if anything worthy of praise, dwell on these things.*
PHILIPPIANS 4:8 NASB

With all the daily messes that make up motherhood, it can be hard to focus on what is good. If you are intentional though and look for the things that are right and true, I'm telling you, it will bless you!

You will begin to realize how much good there really is in the crazy world of mothering. Seriously!

There are people I have placed in your life who will make your day today. Some will be complete strangers. They will do one nice thing for you, and you will not see them again until eternity. Others are people who are your friends and neighbors who care for you. Of course there are your children who say the sweetest things and warm your heart. Write these down when you can and remember them.

There is beauty I have placed all around you. Stop. Look. It's all over the place in My vast creation. Enjoy it today!

*Father God, thank You for all that is good in my life! Thank You for my children and all that You are doing for us. Amen.*

# WISE COUNSEL FOR MAMA

*A wise man is strong, and a man of knowledge*
*increases power. For by wise guidance you will wage war,*
*and in abundance of counselors there is victory.*
PROVERBS 24:5–6 NASB

Real wisdom comes from God. You know, from My Father, the Holy Spirit, and Me. You will need it as a mother. You know that, of course! So ask for it often, and then you will be able to wisely apply your growing knowledge.

Don't be afraid to ask for advice from others you have seen live wisely in Me. In fact, ask a group of these people and you will have a wealth of good thinking that will help you make better decisions.

People who neglect to seek advice and charge ahead with only their thinking often lose out. They let their pride get in the way and miss many victories because of it. You can do better. Wisdom and wise counsel await you; go get them both, sweet woman whom I love!

*Lord, give me wisdom for today, and show me those whom*
*I should seek counsel from as I seek to be the best mother*
*I can be for these children You have entrusted to me. Amen.*

# SOUL SWEETNESS

*Pleasant words are a honeycomb, sweet*
*to the soul and healing to the bones.*
PROVERBS 16:24 NASB

My words for you are profitable and forward moving. Try to let your words be this way, too, as much as you possibly can.

When you speak positively and lovingly, you speak life into others. Think of it—your children will grow under encouraging words just as flowers respond to water and sunshine. Upwardly getting stronger, they will send down healthy roots and display beautiful growth at the same time.

Even when delivering discipline to your children, you can speak with love and they will not question your heart for them. Every chance you get, offer words that are affirming and kind. You'll be surprised how fewer frowns there will be, how much anger is defused, how many low spirits are lifted, including yours! Before you know it, your sweet words will bring a blessing back to you in unexpected ways.

Even your health will benefit from speaking positive words. It affects all of you and those around you wonderfully!

*Lord God, help me speak life into those around me, including*
*myself, that I would reflect You as light and salt in the lives*
*of my children and all those I encounter today. Amen.*

# STRENGTH IN HIS WORD

*"Only be strong and very courageous; be careful to do according
to all the law which Moses My servant commanded you; do not
turn from it to the right or to the left, so that you may have
success wherever you go. . .for then you will make your
way prosperous, and then you will have success."*

Joshua 1:7–8 NASB

What is it that you most need to be strong in today with mothering your children? I know the answer, but I want you to think about this for yourself.

There are many things you are learning and teaching your children every day. My Word will be a constant guide for you. Keep going with it, and find what you need so you can do your best for them. You will excel as a mother this way, I promise you!

Whether it is discipline or encouragement, grace or selflessness, perseverance or self-control, perhaps discernment or service, any or all of these your children may need to observe and absorb. Now, there's a challenge!

In Me you are strong every day. You can do this!

*Lord, thank You for Your Word! Show me today exactly
what I need to train my children in Your wisdom. Amen.*

# LEAN NOT ON YOURSELF

*Lean on, trust in, and be confident in the Lord with all your heart
and mind and do not rely on your own insight or understanding.
In all your ways know, recognize, and acknowledge Him,
and He will direct and make straight and plain your paths.*
PROVERBS 3:5–6 AMP

I t may sound cliché, like the easy answer for how to best live—to trust Me with all your heart. But when it comes to your everyday living, you know just how hard it is!

You have been made with a great mind, so you can be quick to think you know what to do and that you know what's best. The Enemy will try to use all the great things My Father made against you by twisting things just right. So don't be fooled!

Trust Me in this great job of motherhood. Keep giving your heart over to Me, and when you need to make a decision, ask Me for direction. I'll give it to you every time.

In your thoughts, in your heart, with your words, and with your actions—just keep working at looking to Me first. You'll be amazed at how much better things will be for you and for your children.

*Dear God, thank You that I can trust You with my
heart! Give me the guidance I need this day to be the
mom I must be for these precious little ones. Amen.*

# BETTER THAN CHRISTMAS MORNING

*For it is by free grace (God's unmerited favor) that you are saved (delivered from judgment and made partakers of Christ's salvation) through [your] faith. And this [salvation] is not of yourselves [of your own doing, it came not through your own striving], but it is the gift of God.*
EPHESIANS 2:8 AMP

The greatest of all gifts: your salvation! I gladly sacrificed so this could be offered with no strings attached. Entirely free to you—I paid for it so you could be with Me in eternity.

It will be easy to forget that this gift comes with absolutely no ties to it. Because you want to serve Me and do the right things, you can easily fall into basing salvation on what you do. Make no such mistake.

For the sake of your children and those you love, make sure you tell them with all the grace you can that their actions do not determine their eternal destiny. Their relationship with Me does.

There's so much freedom in this attitude. You will stop judging others and yourself. You will live under grace and reflect grace. It's beautiful!

*Lord, help me to reflect Your grace today so my children will eagerly accept the biggest and best gift of all: You! Amen.*

# ANSWERS

*"Thus says the LORD who made the earth, the LORD who formed it to establish it, the LORD is His name, 'Call to Me and I will answer you, and I will tell you great and mighty things, which you do not know.'"*
JEREMIAH 33:2–3 NASB

I know there are countless questions you will want the answers to. Many of them will not be fully answered in this earthly life, but I want you to know that many can be!

I want to give you truth and help you uncover what you need to be the best person and most excellent mother you can be. So ask Me all the questions you want!

Then be prepared to listen. It can be hard to hear at times in the chaos of life, but something will come. As you know, sometimes the answer will simply be no. This can be very difficult to accept. I know.

At times the silence may seem cruel to you, but trust Me. The answers are often delivered in unexpected ways, but I promise—I will give you exactly what you need.

I love your questions and am endlessly creative. I have such great conversations about you with My Father and the Holy Spirit. There are wonderful things in store for you!

*Lord God, give me the answers I need for today,
and help me to trust You with every answer,
even when it's not what I thought
it should be. Amen.*

# SO BLESSED

*Behold, children are a gift of the LORD, the fruit of the womb is a reward. Like arrows in the hand of a warrior, so are the children of one's youth. How blessed is the man whose quiver is full of them.*
PSALM 127:3–5 NASB

Your children are a blessing. I know you know that. But let's be honest, there are days when you wonder, aren't there? Days when things seem off kilter, when the timing of everything feels wrong. Days when your kids—well, let's just say it, they don't always *feel* like a blessing to you. You're human. They're human. It's not an easy road!

On these days, even if it's only for short moments, focus on the beauty of your children. Think on the sweet and funny things they say and do. Marvel at their innocence and curiosity—their incredible capacity for learning! Capture these moments any way you can, in writing or with photos. Admire your little ones while they're sleeping, and pray for the day ahead.

Remember that I love them even more than you do. That's hard to imagine, isn't it?

*Lord, thank You for my children! Bless this day with beautiful moments that reflect Your goodness. Amen.*

# GOOD HABITS

*All discipline for the moment seems not to be joyful, but sorrowful;*
*yet to those who have been trained by it, afterwards it yields*
*the peaceful fruit of righteousness. Therefore, strengthen the*
*hands that are weak and the knees that are feeble.*
HEBREWS 12:11–12 NASB

The structure and boundaries you are giving your children have many layers. Some are simple physical things to keep them healthy and safe, while others will train them up for mental and spiritual growth.

It's all very important, of course. And all along, aren't you learning, too? I want you to know that I smile through this whole process. It is a beautiful thing!

Every bit of discipline that you teach and reinforce with care for your children will benefit them beyond their comprehension. But even you will be surprised by the results. So keep up the good work. Strengthen your children with healthy boundaries and daily practices that will help them become strong. In the process, you are getting stronger, too!

*Lord God, thank You for Your guidance that allows me to guide*
*my children in the same ways. Give me the energy and wisdom*
*to provide all they need to be strong people*
*for Your glory. Amen.*

# ETERNAL IMPACT

*For momentary, light affliction is producing for us an eternal weight of glory far beyond all comparison, while we look not at the things which are seen, but at the things which are not seen; for the things which are seen are temporal, but the things which are not seen are eternal.*

2 CORINTHIANS 4:17–18 NASB

In the many daily tasks that fill your time as a mother, you strive to do the best for your children each and every day. That is obvious. I see it.

Some of your trials are exhausting, and you may start to wonder why you have to endure so much, but I promise you—there is great reward for all of your efforts!

It can be hard to imagine beyond the things you see and walk through now in this earthly life. But I want to give you glimpses of eternity, the things you cannot see right now. What you are doing today, even the little things, it all makes an impact on eternity. The way you love your children ripples off to the way your whole family loves others. You are impacting so many in powerful ways.

It's mysterious, I know, but one day it will be crystal clear.

*Lord, give me the endurance to persevere. Help me remember that You are making beauty from what can feel ugly to me at times. I give You this day. Amen.*

# JOY IN DREAMS

*Hope deferred makes the heart sick; but when*
*dreams come true at last, there is life and joy.*
PROVERBS 13:12 TLB

I want you to know that there is always hope! No matter what you are going through with your children, hope remains.

There are times when you need to see it to keep going. You can be sure that My Father will continue to give you a taste of your dreams and desires so that discouragement doesn't creep in and darken you.

I want to encourage you to do this in actions, too. You can work toward a desire of yours or help your children do this. It may be a small project that you really want to accomplish. Use the creativity you've been given, and do it! You will feel a lively satisfaction and give your kids a small picture of how God is working on things for you in much bigger ways.

My Father has given you dreams and desires for a reason. Keep seeking Our guidance, and keep growing. Watch patiently, and see how it all comes together.

*Father God, I give You my desires today. I know not everything*
*I dream of may be realized in this earthly life, but I ask for Your hand*
*on the dreams I should pursue, that I would glorify You. Amen.*

# FAITH IN THE CREATOR

*Now faith is confidence in what we hope for and assurance about
what we do not see. This is what the ancients were commended for.
By faith we understand that the universe was formed at God's command,
so that what is seen was not made out of what was visible.*

HEBREWS 11:1–3 NIV

You believe, even on the darkest days. You know that I am with you and that all I have promised is true. No matter the measure of your faith, it is so beautiful to Me!

You hear from the faithful that I will not forsake you and your children, that the great eternal promises will be fulfilled. Hang on to every bit of that Good News validated in My Word; it's absolutely true!

What I created (well, along with My Father and the Holy Spirit) is so incredibly vast that it's impossible for the human mind to begin to comprehend it. We spoke it all into being, and what a great time that was and still is! The best part was when We made you and your brothers and sisters in Our image. There are countless people, yet I know each and every one ever made or to be formed.

When you, My dear child, are counted among those with faith, I couldn't be more thrilled!

*Lord, You are amazing! Thank You for giving me faith
in the unseen. I put my trust in You this day. Amen.*

# RENEWAL ABOUNDS

*"Forget the former things; do not dwell on the past. See, I am doing a new thing! Now it springs up; do you not perceive it? I am making a way in the wilderness and streams in the wasteland."*
ISAIAH 43:18–19 NIV

The Enemy of your soul likes to remind you of your past, which, by the way, includes the slipup that may have happened just a minute ago. But I'm telling you, do not let your mind stay on these things!

I want to remind you to move forward in forgiveness and grace. I gave My life so you could have this. I really want you to avail yourself of it! Remember that I'm constantly building and blessing My dear children—you!

Brand new places are being formed every moment, beautiful spots in barren spaces. I have great plans for you. So keep looking for the renewal. You will find it—it is in My creation all around, it is in you, it is in your children and in your closest relationships. Renewal is available through Me every day, every minute. Look for that.

*Father God, thank You that You remember not my sin. Renew my heart and mind today. Amen.*

# BEAUTY DAY BY DAY

*Therefore we do not lose heart. Though outwardly we are
wasting away, yet inwardly we are being renewed day by day.*

2 CORINTHIANS 4:16 NIV

Being a mom takes its physical toll on you every day, and I know there are many times when you look in the mirror and see that. It's no secret that you will decline physically as you age, but somehow it sneaks up on you, doesn't it?

I want you to know that while you can only limit the physical wear and tear, you are stronger and stronger internally as you grow in your knowledge of Me.

Keep focusing on the Good News of the Gospel, on grace, and on how I rose from the dead! Strengthen your heart with this, and share it with your children, family, friends, and neighbors—so that they too may come to know My saving grace.

Focus on the eternal beautiful life you will have with Me, rather than on the decay that occurs in this life, and you will encourage many others to share this hope with you, too, including your precious children!

*Lord, thank You that I do not need to worry about the physical
fading that is sure to happen in motherhood. Turn my eyes to
eternal things that I may be beautiful in Your sight. Amen.*

# MOMMY TIME-OUT. . .IN THE BATHROOM

*But the fruit of the [Holy] Spirit [the work which His presence*
*within accomplishes] is love, joy (gladness), peace, patience*
*(an even temper, forbearance), kindness, goodness (benevolence),*
*faithfulness, gentleness (meekness, humility), self-control*
*(self-restraint, continence). Against such things there is no law.*
GALATIANS 5:22–23 AMP

This is quite a list of characteristics, isn't it? I want to encourage you right off, these are all things that yielding to the Holy Spirit will begin to produce in you. Not overnight, mind you, so give yourself time. It's a process.

When you come to the end of your patience with your children and self-control becomes an issue, come quickly to Me. You may need to shut the door behind you in the bathroom to get away for a minute and compose yourself, and that's okay! Then pray and listen.

Keep doing this (maybe not always the shutting-yourself-in-the-bathroom part), and little by little you will begin to notice yourself changing and growing. It will come!

*Lord, I yield to You. Right now. I give You this moment*
*and this day. Give me a continual desire to be in the*
*process of being fruitful for You. Amen.*

# THE GROWING PROCESS

*Guide older women into lives of reverence so they end up as neither gossips nor drunks, but models of goodness. By looking at them, the younger women will know how to love their husbands and children, be virtuous and pure, keep a good house, be good wives. We don't want anyone looking down on God's Message because of their behavior.*
TITUS 2:3–5 MSG

Do you have an older woman in your life to model yourself after in your life of faith? If not, find one, and find a good one. Someone who loves Me and is striving to grow in Me, as well as someone who is honest about her struggles. You will find great benefit in your life as a mother by doing this. You can see how others have made it through tough times and learn from their mothering.

You will grow in your faith by being around someone more mature than you. It's so good to do this, and you'll end up thoroughly enjoying a mentor friendship like this.

Before you know it, you will see how you can help someone needing reinforcement on the journey, maybe a college–aged girl who needs encouragement or a brand-new mom. It's not about trying to be perfect for her; it's about encouraging one another along the way.

*Lord, show me women ahead of me and behind me on the faith path, and give me the courage to learn from and encourage those in these roles. Amen.*

# EVERYDAY SACRIFICE

*Through Him then, let us continually offer up a sacrifice*
*of praise to God, that is, the fruit of lips that give thanks*
*to His name. And do not neglect doing good and*
*sharing, for with such sacrifices God is pleased.*
HEBREWS 13:15–16 NASB

You give up so much as a mother for the sake of your children. I want to applaud how you put yourself aside in so many ways. Not to the point of neglect, mind you, but to the extent that you point your children to Me and the sacrifice I made for them, and for you.

When your kids see your selflessness and all that you give in love, you are showing them a tangible example of Me. In this way you can lay out a measure of the Gospel story for them with your everyday life.

Experiencing sacrificial love given on their behalf is powerful. Receiving grace freely given in exchange for nothing—well, you're living it out with this one!

My love is going to shine through you, and your children will know who I am.

*Lord, give me the strength and faith I need today to sacrifice*
*with love for my children, that I would reflect You. Amen.*

# MY STRENGTH

*Therefore I am well content with weaknesses, with insults,*
*with distresses, with persecutions, with difficulties,*
*for Christ's sake; for when I am weak, then I am strong.*
2 Corinthians 12:10 nasb

There are certainly weaknesses and distresses that make you feel weak as a mom, aren't there? I know it's hard to be okay with areas of life where you feel you come up short. Or with a trying situation you suddenly find yourself in, especially when your children may be impacted.

Here's the good news: whatever it is, I can be your strength. I can make up the difference between your shortfalls and your successes as a parent, no matter the cause. You may or may not have a long-term thorn in the flesh like my friend Paul did, but either way, if you depend on Me, you are going to be strong. I'm not saying not to work on getting better at things, but in times of weakness, I want you to always remember who I am.

You will begin to see these times as a gift because you will be drawn to Me in them and you will find sweet covering that only I can provide.

*Lord, I see my shortcomings every day. I need You to be my strength*
*today. Enable me to be the mother You want me to be. Amen.*

# THANKFUL

*Therefore, since we receive a kingdom which cannot be shaken, let us show gratitude, by which we may offer to God an acceptable service with reverence and awe.*
HEBREWS 12:28 NASB

The more you can point out the things you are thankful for, the happier you are going to be. And I have to say, it is beautiful to see gratitude!

So name the things you are thankful for in front of your children and with your children. They will develop a sweet, appreciative attitude from this practice. There is so much to name—think about it. Your family, your home, your friends, your food, the many opportunities you have—the list is long!

Not the least of the items to give praise for is the immovable eternal kingdom you are a part of as one of My children. Share this with your kids. You will offer great hope for tomorrow and joy for today.

*Lord, I am so grateful for Your love and eternal plan with great promise. Give me the clarity today to focus on what I am thankful for. Amen.*

# SPIRIT LIFT

*Pray hard and long. Pray for your brothers and sisters.*
*Keep your eyes open. Keep each other's spirits up*
*so that no one falls behind or drops out.*
EPHESIANS 6:18 MSG

In your journey as a mother, there are many others alongside you who need your prayers and encouragement. You may easily notice your children's prayer needs but maybe not so easily your friends' or neighbors'.

It takes intentionality and alertness, really looking around in your everyday life to see the needs of others. But when you do this, you will be amazed at how much praying for or speaking kinds words to others will lift you up at the same time. You will feel good about helping in some way.

The other thing that will often surprise you is how much the people you forgot you helped will be there for you when you need it. Not that this is your motive to help them, but it just ends up blessing you back a hundredfold.

Every time you speak love into the lives of others, and to your children, you are making Me more real to them. It's beautiful!

*Dear God, give me eyes to see the needs around me*
*and a willingness to reach out as I should,*
*that I would reflect You today. Amen.*

# IT ALL COUNTS

*But thanks be to God, who gives us the victory through our*
*Lord Jesus Christ. Therefore, my beloved brethren, be steadfast,*
*immovable, always abounding in the work of the Lord,*
*knowing that your toil is not in vain in the Lord.*
1 CORINTHIANS 15:57–58 NASB

How many tasks do you complete every day as a mother that feel like striving after the wind? A lot, I know!

There are so many repetitive chores. It may seem like doing these one more time will not make a difference. You may get to thinking, *Why do I bother?*

But just hang on—I have encouraging news for you! I want you to know that not a single small thing that you do when you are looking to glorify Me in your work will be wasted. Not one.

I am the Master of using every little thing. All the menial jobs. The breakfasts, lunches, and dinners that blur together. The mountains of laundry and revolving door of dirt. The countless settling of arguments and calming of fears. All of these add up to something absolutely beautiful as you invest in the hearts and souls of your children. You pour into them love and sacrifice that are a reflection of Me.

*Lord, today help me to push past the feelings of futility*
*that nag at me so that I can see the bigger picture*
*of mothering in a way that shines for You. Amen.*

# PRECIOUS LIFE

*The Lord God who created the heavens and stretched them out, who created the earth and everything in it, who gives life and breath and spirit to everyone in all the world, he is the one who says to his Servant, the Messiah: "I the Lord have called you to demonstrate my righteousness."*
ISAIAH 42:5–6 TLB

You know how you love to watch your children sleep? The rise and fall of their chests as they breathe peacefully is so precious. I know; I feel the same way about them and about you.

Your life is a masterpiece. It started with creating you and has continued with each breath. Now that you're a mother, so much beauty is unfolding as your children grow, and I am loving watching it all!

The way you love them and expand your faith is awesome. As you see them step out into places outside of home, it feels like your heart is out there walking around with legs.

That's how I feel about you.

*Lord, thank You for each breath and for the great love You give my children and I. Help me not to take a moment for granted today. Amen.*

# STRONG MOTHERS

*Finally, be strong in the Lord and in the strength of his might. Put on the whole armor of God, that you may be able to stand against the schemes of the devil.*
EPHESIANS 6:10–11 ESV

When you feel weak, I can give you all the strength you need and more, and I'm so happy to do this for you!

Your children and the many demands of life may be wearing you out in a thousand ways today, but I want to help you. I love you and your children like crazy, and your work as a parent is so vital.

I have a motherhood arsenal of armor that is at your disposal. First of all, make it a daily practice to build yourself up in truth so that the lies of the Enemy won't stand a chance on you. Your faith will be a shield for you, protecting you from the Enemy's attacks. Your only offensive weapon is the sword of My Word, My message, given to you by the Holy Spirit (Ephesians 6:14–17). Keep using this armor, and teach your children to use it, too. In Me, you can be a strong family.

*Lord God, I am weak in the face of all that is in front of me today. Give me strength by being my strength, that I would be the mother You would have me be today for my children. Amen.*

# ENCOURAGMENT FOR ALL

*Let us hold unswervingly to the hope we profess, for he who promised
is faithful. And let us consider how we may spur one another on toward
love and good deeds, not giving up meeting together, as some are in
the habit of doing, but encouraging one another.*
HEBREWS 10:23–25 NIV

The hope you have in Me is a very real thing; remembering this will get you through a lot!

The challenges of motherhood, the decisions you have to make, and the physical and emotional energy you exert daily can wear you right out. You could start to feel alone and discouraged, but don't fall into that trap!

There are other moms all around you with similar struggles, and I want to use you and your Christian sisters to encourage one another in your faith. So when you feel a bit overwhelmed and want to turn inward with sadness, resist.

Reach out instead. What you will find is that you will be just as blessed by others as they are by you. Okay, maybe not by everyone! Be persistent and patient in this. Find other moms at church, play groups, or Bible study. Be a part of Christian community in your daily and weekly life. You and your kids will be so glad you did!

*Lord, give me the strength and courage to reach out to
others, that I would be a blessing to them and to You. Amen.*

# ENTRUSTED FULLY TO YOU

*The Lord is my light and my salvation—whom shall I fear?*
*The Lord is the stronghold of my life—of whom shall I be afraid?*
*When the wicked advance against me to devour me, it is my*
*enemies and my foes who will stumble and fall.*

PSALM 27:1–2 NIV

The force that stands on your behalf is mighty! Of this you can be absolutely certain. It may not always look this way to you, but trust Me. I am for you, and there is no one who can stand against Me.

So when you may be fearful for yourself or for your children, know that you can trust Me with all of it. The concerns you have for your children can be especially great. When they are out of your sight or battling an issue that is out of your control, it can be scary. But know this—every aspect of their well-being can be entrusted to My care. No matter what they do or where they go, I am able to protect them. Keep lifting them up to Me.

*Lord God, today I give You my children. I entrust*
*their complete care to You, the only One who can*
*fully protect and bless them. Amen.*

# EVERYDAY OFFERING

*So here's what I want you to do, God helping you: Take your everyday, ordinary life—your sleeping, eating, going-to-work, and walking-around life—and place it before God as an offering. Embracing what God does for you is the best thing you can do for him.*
ROMANS 12:1 MSG

My dear friend Paul says it well in this passage. It really is the simple acts in your normal life that I want to use, whatever normal is for you.

A regular day for you with the kids can mean running at breakneck speed after a sleepless night or enjoying a nice breakfast in your pj's with the kids saying adorable things that make you love life. It could be a day when the house is a real train wreck or a day when you are feeling really on top of things. It might be a packed day from 6:00 a.m. to 6:00 p.m., only to get home for your second shift of work at home, or a day you're home all day with the kids just relaxing and playing together.

You know how far the pendulum can swing; you don't know what a day will bring. But it's your regular day I can use for great things, one regular thing at a time. Whatever it is—I love when you give it to Me.

*Lord, I give You the normal of this day, as crazy or as calm as it may be. Make my ordinary extraordinary. Amen.*

# SEEING AND BEING IN HIM

*Don't become so well-adjusted to your culture that you fit into it without even thinking. Instead, fix your attention on God. You'll be changed from the inside out. Readily recognize what he wants from you, and quickly respond to it. Unlike the culture around you, always dragging you down to its level of immaturity, God brings the best out of you, develops well-formed maturity in you.*

ROMANS 12:2 MSG

You help your children to adjust well to a lot of things, or at least you try. This is all well and good unless you're not careful.

When it comes to your culture, be especially watchful. There are so many subtle things that seek to pull you and your children in. But if you just keep putting My Word up next to these things, you will know where it's great to fit in and where it really isn't. Teach your children the truth, and encourage them toward good decisions.

You'll get to praise them for good choices, but you will likely also help them adjust to not always being in the crowd they thought was cool. But you get it; it happens to you, too.

They will learn, just as you are learning, to love like I do and grow in faith and wisdom, becoming strong people who shine for Me.

*Lord, give me clarity today to see and be in You. Amen.*

# LIVING IN GRACE

*I'm speaking to you out of deep gratitude for all that God has
given me, and especially as I have responsibilities in relation to you.
Living then, as every one of you does, in pure grace, it's important
that you not misinterpret yourselves as people who are bringing
this goodness to God. No, God brings it all to you.*

ROMANS 12:3 MSG

You try to live your life well, in a way that is pleasing to Me. This can get misconstrued into a belief that somehow My love and grace can be earned. But that would be the opposite of grace.

So don't get confused! Because of what I have done for you by dying on the cross and rising from the dead, there is no act that needs to be done to get to Me. No supermom behavior or church volunteering or following all the rules. None of that.

Rather, it's simple faith, a posture of the heart.

Because the work that earned your grace is done—you get to live in Me, and as a result you will want to do what is good and true.

*Lord God, let me abide in You this day, that I may live in grace and
offer grace, genuinely desiring to do what is good and true. Amen.*